This is a fictionalised biography describing some of the key moments (so far!) in the career of Chloe Kelly.

Some of the events described in this book are based upon the author's imagination and are probably not entirely accurate representations of what actually happened.

Tales from the Pitch
Chloe Kelly
by Robin Adams

Published by Raven Books
An imprint of Ransom Publishing Ltd.
Unit 7, Brocklands Farm, West Meon, Hampshire GU32 1JN, UK
www.ransom.co.uk

ISBN   978 180047 693 6
First published in 2023

Copyright © 2023 Ransom Publishing Ltd.
Text copyright © 2023 Ransom Publishing Ltd.
Cover illustration by Ben Farr © 2023 Ben Farr

A CIP catalogue record of this book is available from the British Library.

All rights reserved. No part of this publication may be reproduced, stored in a retrieval system, or transmitted, in any form or by any means, electronic, mechanical, photocopying, recording or otherwise, without the prior permission of the publishers.

The rights of Robin Adams to be identified as the author and of Ben Farr to be identified as the illustrator of this Work have been asserted by them in accordance with sections 77 and 78 of the Copyright, Design and Patents Act 1988.

TALES FROM THE PITCH

CHLOE KELLY

ROBIN ADAMS

RAVEN

CONTENTS

		Page
1	The Winner	7
2	In the Cages	18
3	"We're Barely Even Winning!"	23
4	Seeing Clearly	28
5	A Few Firsts	33
6	On Loan	38
7	Waiting for the Future	42
8	Welcome Home	46
9	Hat-Trick Heroine	52
10	Permanent	59
11	Emphatic	67
12	Sidelined	74
13	Rejuvenated	79
14	Scintillating Form	85
15	The Future is Bright	93
16	ACL	99
17	Back in Style	105
18	Lioness	113

1
THE WINNER

July 2022, Wembley Stadium, London, England
Euro 2022 Final, England v Germany

"Slow down – now breathe." Lucy Bronze caught Chloe's eye as she spoke to her. "Don't worry – you'll get your chance to show what you can do out there. The gaffer knows how hard you've worked to get here."

It helped, but it didn't stop Chloe Kelly pacing anxiously around the Lionesses' dressing room. The kick-off in the final of Euro 2022 was fast approaching, and she was restless. She tried to use the deafening noise of the Euros-record crowd of 87,192 fans to help her focus her thoughts.

England had fought hard to get here, battling past Austria, Norway, and Northern Ireland in the group stage. They'd gone on to beat Spain 2-1 in a close-fought quarter-final, then thrashed Sweden 4-0 in the semis. Now they faced England's old football rivals, Germany.

England had played as a tight unit, following the disciplined, attacking style of their manager, Sarina Wiegman, who'd won the previous Euros with her native country, the Netherlands.

England were in great form. So why was Chloe feeling so nervous?

Sarina had started every match in the tournament with the same starting line-up. This had given England real consistency, but it had only given Chloe short stints coming off the bench, late in games. She knew that the final would be no different – and she worried that she might not have enough time to make an impact.

Chloe thought back over the past year, and all she'd been through to get here. After suffering an ACL injury in a league game for her club, Man City, she'd been working feverishly to get fit in time for the Euros. The injury had cost her the chance to play for Great Britain at the Tokyo Olympics, and had very nearly cost her a spot in the England Euros squad.

But, against the odds, she'd fought her way back. In fact, she'd spent a lot of time in the gym, working on her recovery alongside Lucy Bronze, the England veteran – and her club team-mate – who'd been recovering from an injury herself. Chloe and Lucy knew each other well. They knew how and when to support each other.

Chloe's thoughts were suddenly interrupted by Sarina, who beckoned the players over to hear her final instructions.

"Today, you have the chance to make history," she began. "Germany have won this tournament eight times. Today, they are expected to win it for a ninth time. It is your job to stop them." Her words echoed around a now-silent dressing room.

"This is our chance to get revenge for 2009," Jill Scott added. She remembered, better than anyone, how it felt to lose to Germany, having done so in that 2009 Euros final.

"Be fearless," Sarina continued. "You know how we play. We must be defensively rigid, but we attack with freedom. I want you to go out and play as if this is any other game. If you do that, Germany will have no chance."

Despite her manager's words, Chloe still felt apprehensive. Sarina's plan didn't include Chloe from the outset. She'd have to hope she was subbed on.

Sensing the self-doubt in her star forward, Sarina approached Chloe.

"Make no mistake, Chloe, your job today is vital," she said with conviction. "You'll come into the game as soon as the Germany defenders begin to tire. That'll be when they're at their most vulnerable – it'll give you the chance to use your pace against them."

"I'll do my best, gaffer," Chloe replied, reassured by the vote of confidence from her manager.

Minutes later, the England players were out on the pitch, the greetings and national anthems already over. As the players took up their positions for the kick-off, Chloe made her way to the bench with the other subs.

"Popp is out injured already," Ella Toone shouted to Chloe, struggling to make herself heard over the deafening roar of the crowd, even though she was sitting right next to Chloe on the bench.

Alexandra Popp, Germany's top scorer of the tournament and their most lethal striker, had been forced to pull out of the squad after an injury in the warm-up.

"Maybe today really is going to be our day," Chloe replied to Ella nervously.

The opening minutes of the game were scrappy, with chances missed and unsuccessful penalty appeals by both sides. There were yellow cards for England players Ellen White and Georgia Stanway too. Both teams were struggling to create clear opportunities.

Then Germany won a corner and, as the ball fizzed in from the left, it caused panic in the England penalty area. Limbs seemed to be flying everywhere, until finally the keeper, Mary Earps, emerged with the ball.

"That was too close," Chloe said to Ella. "They're all over us."

"They need us out there *now*," Ella added. "We're getting trapped in our own half."

Fortunately, England weathered the early storm and at half-time the game was level at 0-0.

In the England dressing room, Chloe looked around at her team-mates' faces. She could see that nerves had begun to creep in. Sarina must have seen this too, as she beckoned the players over to her.

"Did you think this would be easy?" she asked them, looking around the room. "England have never beaten Germany in the Euros before. They were expecting this to be a comfortable win."

She let her words sink in before continuing. "Nil-nil is a good first half. Remember – we have a plan. We have subs to bring on who can now win us this game. We've done the hard defending – now we attack."

Chloe knew that, for the second half, she was a key part of the manager's plan. She was ready for it – the most important game of her career so far.

Back out on the pitch, Chloe and Ella made their way back to the bench. But this time, Chloe knew it wouldn't be for long.

Germany had made one substitution at half-time, bringing on Tabea Waßmuth for Jule Brand. This seemed to buoy the visitors, and they started the second half with renewed determination. Tackles flew in and shots skewed wide – until the game once again became bogged down in stalemate.

Ten minutes into the second half, and needing inspiration, Sarina turned to her bench.

"Ella! Alessia! Get over here – you're going on."

Ella Toone and Alessia Russo were strong, attacking players. Chloe knew that, if anybody could turn the tide of the game, it would be them.

Sure enough, Ella quickly made an impact. Just seven minutes after coming on, Keira Walsh played a beautiful through-ball over the top, breaking the Germany lines. Ella was on to it in a flash. She took one touch, before lobbing the ball over the stranded keeper and into the net.

GOAL!

The England fans in the stadium erupted, an immense wall of noise rising from the record crowd. Chloe leapt up from the bench to celebrate, now desperate to get onto the pitch and join in.

Her chance came sooner than she expected. Beth

Mead had been injured shortly before the goal and couldn't continue, so Chloe found herself standing on the touchline, waiting for the fourth official to raise her number on the board.

Sarina shouted one last instruction. "Be patient, Chloe. The defenders will continue to tire – make the most of your chances."

With sixty-three minutes on the clock, Chloe had half an hour to do just that.

England naturally fell back after taking the lead, which meant that Chloe didn't get much time on the ball. She danced past defenders and sprayed passes to her team-mates, but the passes were smothered quickly and didn't amount to much.

The clock was winding down and it looked as if England would hold on for a 1-0 win. But then, with just ten minutes to go, disaster struck.

The German substitute, Waßmuth, broke down the right wing and played an accurate cross to the left foot of Lina Magull, who slammed it into the roof of the net. Germany were level.

The final ten minutes passed by uneventfully, with

neither team willing to risk losing the game by trying to win it.

At the full-time whistle, the exhausted England players regrouped on the touchline with the coaches.

"Forget about their goal," their captain, Leah Williamson, told them. "No use dwelling on it. Germany have spent all their energy getting level. Now this is our game to win. And we have extra time to do it in."

As the first half of extra time began, Chloe knew that she would have more chances to make an impact. Leah was right – Germany had tired, and were struggling to keep up with her.

Time after time, Chloe darted in from the wings, wreaking havoc in the Germany midfield, but somehow she couldn't find a way through. As the first half of extra time ended, the game was still in the balance.

Then, with just ten minutes left on the clock, everything changed.

England had a corner on the right-hand side. Chloe's team-mate at Man City, Lauren Hemp, whipped the ball in with her left foot, and the crowd held their breath as the ball sailed into the box, causing the Germany defenders to scramble. They failed to deal with the ball, and it bounced off Lucy Bronze. Everyone reacted slowly to the bounce – except for Chloe.

She forced her way past the defender to reach the ball, turning towards goal and shielding it as she did so. She swung desperately at the ball with her right foot, but didn't connect with it.

Ordinarily the chance would have been gone, but Chloe was no ordinary player. Before any of the defenders could react, she pounced on the ball and poked it under the keeper.

GOAL!

Time suddenly seemed to stand still. Overcome with emotion, Chloe checked that the goal had been given, then whipped off her shirt and, whirling it above her head, sprinted towards the fans. She was soon mobbed by her team-mates, who were equally stunned by what she'd just done.

In the aftermath of the goal, the referee gave Chloe a yellow card for "excessive celebration", but Chloe was beyond caring. This was the best moment of her football career – and the best yellow card she'd ever received.

The final ten minutes seemed to pass by in a blur, but England defended well and saw the game out comfortably.

At the full-time whistle, the magnitude of what the players had achieved began to sink in. England were now European Champions – and had won it at Wembley, the home of English football.

It had been in front of the biggest-ever crowd for a Euros game, and against arch-rivals Germany as well.

Chloe had scored the winning goal in the final of the Euros and, in doing so, she'd become one of the world's most iconic players.

As Chloe stood on the pitch, looking around at her team-mates and the cheering fans, she thought back to the long journeys as a child, spent getting to the Arsenal academy. All her sacrifices over the years had been worth it, if only just for this moment.

In that moment, Chloe knew that she'd become an inspiration to so many young girls everywhere.

But for her, this was just another step on her journey to become the best.

2
IN THE CAGES

May 2005, Hanwell, London, England

"Are you playing with us, Chloe?" her brother, Jack, called out from across the park.

"Yes! Don't start without me!" she replied eagerly.

Chloe had recently started playing football with her brothers and their friends. She was only seven years old, younger than the others, but the boys treated her no differently. And Chloe couldn't get enough of it.

She was one of seven children in her family. With five football-mad older brothers, it was inevitable that she'd be exposed to a lot of football, but her eagerness to join in had surprised even her family.

That morning, her sister, Paris, had watched Chloe pulling her QPR kit out of the cupboard.

"You're not going to play football again, are you?"

Paris already knew the answer, but she couldn't quite believe how much her sister had become obsessed with the game.

"Why do you like it anyway?" Paris added. "It just looks sweaty and tiring to me."

"It *is* sweaty and tiring. But it's not *just* those things," Chloe answered. "I want to be like Bobby Zamora or Kelly Smith when I grow up. How can I do that without getting sweaty and tired?"

Chloe's five brothers – Jack, Daniel, and triplets Ryan, Jamie and Martin – knew better than to say no to their sister. She was at least as keen on football as they were. And besides, Chloe made up the numbers to a nice even six players. Perfect for three v three.

Chloe sprinted across the park to where Jack and the

others were waiting for her. They were at the Windmill Park cages, near their housing estate in West London. This was no Wembley – just a hard slab of concrete, fenced on all sides.

But that made no difference to Chloe. She'd been kicking a ball about from the moment she could walk and, now that she could play with her brothers, her love of the game had reached new heights.

"You're out of breath already!" Jack remarked, as she reached her brothers.

"I'm just getting warmed up!" Chloe replied, eager to get into the match.

"OK – you all know the rules," Jack continued. "Firm but fair. Not everything is a foul, so if there's a shoulder barge, the game continues. That goes for you too, Chloe."

Chloe received no special treatment from her brothers, which was just how she liked it. They treated her as an equal in every way – and, in football at least, she knew that she was already their equal.

Jack organised the teams. It was going to be the triplets against himself, Chloe, and Daniel.

He booted the ball up in the air and the game was underway. Chloe was quickest to the ball, but was easily barged off it by Jamie.

She knew she couldn't match her brothers' strength, but strength wasn't everything. She was quicker and more agile than any of them – and she was tough too. She wasn't shaken easily by a push or a shove.

Chloe bounced back onto her feet and chased Jamie down before he could get a shot away, sneaking a foot in and dispossessing him easily.

Her brothers were continually caught unawares by just how fast she was, and this element of surprise was proving to be one of her biggest advantages.

"Great job, Chloe!" Daniel called over. "I'm open."

Chloe spotted him off to her right and, after weaving past Martin, she drew Ryan out of goal and deftly passed the ball across to Daniel, for an easy tap-in.

"What a pass, Chloe!" Daniel grinned. "Kelly Smith who? Chloe Kelly is going all the way to the top!"

The game continued at a relentless pace. Everybody was very competitive and nobody wanted to lose. Ultimately Chloe, Daniel and Jack ran out winners – or so Chloe told them. They'd lost count of the score long ago, and were now just playing for the fun of it.

It was the setting sun that finally prompted them to pack it in – it was just getting too dark to see the ball properly.

As they all strolled back home, tired but smiling, Chloe thought more about her love of football. She'd already come so far in her short time playing with her brothers. She knew she had talent and a passion for the game – was it possible she could really make something out of it?

She knew already that the path into women's football was a difficult one. She'd heard stories about the work that players like Kelly Smith had had to put in, just to make a career in football.

Chloe wondered whether she might have what it took to follow in her idol's footsteps.

For now, Chloe was content playing and learning alongside her brothers. But, if the opportunity ever came along, she knew she'd take it in a heartbeat.

3
"WE'RE BARELY EVEN WINNING!"

February 2008, Tottenham, London, England
Home Counties League, Spurs U10 v QPR U10

Chloe woke with a start. It was six o'clock – on matchday. She always woke up early when there was football to play. It was as if she couldn't wait.

But today, she wasn't playing with her brothers in the cages. Today, she was playing for Queens Park Rangers, the club she'd supported her whole life, in a Home Counties League match.

It had been a whirlwind three years for Chloe. She'd been spotted by QPR scouts and had joined their academy, after impressing at a tournament with her school.

She had started playing for the Under-10s team when she was just eight years old. Yet, even with that two-year age difference, Chloe was still able to hold her own and impress the coaches.

Now aged ten and in her final year with the team, she was still showing that she had something special.

QPR had started the season incredibly well, so far scoring 60 goals without conceding one. And Chloe had been an essential part of that success.

But today's opponents, Spurs, would be a tough challenge. They definitely posed the biggest threat to QPR's unbeaten record.

A few hours later, not long before kick-off, Chloe was sitting in the dressing room with the rest of the QPR players, going through their game plan.

"Just go out there and express yourselves, girls," the manager told the players. "Spurs will be stubborn – they'll try to contain you. But they're not going to be able to. I know you're good enough to beat them."

After addressing the team, the manager caught Chloe's eye and came over to speak to her.

"Your pace is just going to be too much for them, Chloe. Go and show everyone why you're such a fantastic player. I know you're going to be moving on soon, but while you're here, let's make the most of it!"

In truth, Chloe didn't need to hear this. She always gave 100% for the team – and today wouldn't be any different.

"Spurs won't know what's hit them!" she replied with a grin.

As the match kicked off, it quickly became clear that Spurs were going to be a serious challenge. They weren't going to go down without a fight.

The early exchanges were mostly even. Chloe tried a few mazy dribbles and played some good passes, but the Spurs defending was resolute and she was limited mostly to long-distance shots.

Then, twenty minutes in, QPR's quality paid off. Chloe danced past the defenders and blazed a shot into the top corner, beating Spurs keeper Renee Lamy.

GOAL!

Despite the goal, Spurs didn't crumble, and instead continued to defend well.

At half-time, it was still 1-0 to QPR. This was something new for the QPR players. After conceding the first goal, most opponents would capitulate and leave huge gaps for QPR to exploit. So, at half-time, QPR often found themselves leading by a large margin.

But, today, Spurs had kept on fighting.

The manager tried to reassure the team. "Well done, girls. Good first half."

"But it's only 1-0. We're barely even winning!" Chloe exclaimed.

"Patience, Chloe," the manager replied with a smile. "You can't always beat teams 5-0 in the first half. There are times in football where you have to slow things down and be more measured. Patience can be just as important as aggression."

This was an approach which Chloe hadn't ever given much thought to. QPR were always best on the front foot, as was she. But she recognised that her manager had a lot more experience than her.

And, anyway, a win was a win. You didn't get more points for spectacular scores.

With this in mind, Chloe started the second half well. She let the Spurs defenders move further up the pitch with the ball, closing them down more cautiously.

As a result, the Spurs players started to relax more – and to make more mistakes. Just five minutes into the second half, QPR had two more goals.

They were now three up. Patience was paying off.

In the end, QPR ran out 7-0 winners, in another emphatic win.

By now, Chloe had become part of a QPR juggernaut. They hadn't been beaten in two years and it was clear that nobody could touch them.

Yet Chloe realised that, even though she loved QPR, her time at the club was coming to an end. To progress as a player – and to forge a path into professional football – she would now need to move elsewhere.

She wondered whether scouts from other clubs had been at today's game.

If so, she was sure that they would have been impressed.

4
SEEING CLEARLY

September 2013, Hanwell, London, England

"Am I too late?" Chloe asked breathlessly.

"Just in time," the ticket inspector at Hanwell railway station replied with a smile.

Chloe smiled with relief. The train to take her to the Arsenal Centre of Excellence would be arriving at any moment. Since moving to Arsenal from QPR, Chloe had been making this journey every day after school.

She had been right in thinking that scouts from other clubs might be watching her. In the end, it was Arsenal who had contacted her parents and offered her a position in their development programme.

Chloe would have liked to have continued at QPR, but she knew that Arsenal gave her opportunities to learn so much more.

"I want to go, Mum, but it's so much further to travel," Chloe had told her mum, Jane, when they'd considered Arsenal's offer. "I'm worried I might not be able to manage the journeys … "

"Don't worry too much about that," Jane had replied enthusiastically. "This is a once-in-a-lifetime opportunity for you. The whole family knows how committed you are to football. You don't want to miss out on something like this – so let's see how it goes."

Chloe had felt reassured by her mum's words. She always had Chloe's best interests at heart, after all.

"Remember all the long days you spent in the park with the boys, when you were only seven?" her mum had added. "If you could do that, then this is just the next step. I believe in you, Chloe."

So, ultimately, Chloe had taken the plunge and joined the bigger club. But, on days like these, waiting on the small platform for her train, with the wind and the rain whipping around her, she wondered whether she'd made the right decision.

She'd established a daily routine for herself after school, and today was no different. She'd made the 25-minute walk from Elthorne Park High School to the railway station, and now she had a few minutes to get her breath back before the train arrived.

Her friends at school couldn't quite understand how – or why – she was so committed to football. All they saw was Chloe getting into school every morning, looking tired from the two-hour round trip – plus the training – of the previous day.

She would get home after training at 11 p.m., and then had to be up for school the next day. But, to Chloe, this routine was a small price to pay for the opportunities that training at Arsenal brought her.

Arsenal had one of the best youth centres for girls' football and, if she could graduate through the system, there was a strong chance of a career in football.

But Chloe knew that nothing was guaranteed. In her time at Arsenal, she'd seen many players dropping out – some who couldn't cope with the travel or the training, and others who'd simply been told that they just weren't good enough.

And yet, Chloe was still there. She was coping with with the travel and the exhausting hours, and her football had seen massive improvements in so many ways. The coaches too seemed very positive.

Just then, a familiar screeching echoed around the station, as the train approached the platform. As it slowed to a halt, Chloe stepped into a carriage and found a seat by the window.

She settled down and began to think about the training session that was coming up. All thoughts of school, the travelling and the cold vanished from her mind. This hour-long journey gave her the opportunity to focus fully on football.

At QPR, Chloe had developed into a player with excellent timing. She knew when to press a defender, when to switch the ball from one foot to the other, and when to throw in a body-feint to keep them all guessing.

Now she was becoming a much more complete forward, excelling in all areas, and was working hard to be more selfless – as happy to be getting an assist as to be scoring a goal herself.

"The train will soon be departing," the guard's voice announced over the intercom.

Chloe stared out of the window as the train began to pull away, rain streaking the window and blurring her view.

But Chloe saw clearly. She'd devoted so much to football and she knew that, at the pace she was going, it was only a matter of time before she'd graduate through the academy and make it to Arsenal's first team.

Comforted by this thought, she settled back into her seat and imagined herself walking out onto the pitch – as a professional Arsenal first-team player.

5
A FEW FIRSTS

July 2015, Meadow Park, Hertfordshire, England
Continental Cup, Arsenal v Watford

"It's only natural to be nervous before your debut, Chloe." Leah Williamson sat down next to Chloe in the dressing room and smiled. "We've all been there."

"I just can't believe it's for real," Chloe said. "I was starting to think it might never happen."

"The manager has seen you play for the Under-17s, and we're all aware of what you can do. It was inevitable that you'd end up playing with us one day!" Leah continued.

It was true. Chloe had established herself firmly in the academy's development squads, even captaining the Under-17 team. But today's game was her first for the senior team. It was a big step up – and Chloe knew just how important it was.

Arsenal were facing Watford, who were in the Women's National League Premier Division, two leagues below the Women's Super League that Arsenal played in.

On paper, that should make Watford easy opponents, but Chloe knew better than to take anything for granted. On top of that, the teams were playing in the Continental Cup, which was famous for its upsets.

Chloe's thoughts were interrupted by the sound of her manager's voice, cutting through the tension.

"Everyone gather round," Pedro Martínez Losa announced, as the players turned to face him. "This is our first chance to show what we're made of in this year's competition. We need to be brave today. Watford are the underdogs – they have nothing to lose. They will come at us hard, and we must be resilient to stop them."

Chloe had spent her years in the Arsenal academy honing exactly these skills. At QPR, she'd already been a skilful and dynamic forward, but she'd always lacked that killer edge, combined with the ability to stand up when her team were on the back foot. Her time with Arsenal had changed all that.

"Most of all, enjoy yourselves," Pedro added. "Play with freedom and take the game to Watford. We have the quality in attack to demolish them. So, today, show me why you should be playing for Arsenal."

Chloe knew that Pedro had been talking about her. She was Arsenal's "quality in attack". Today was her chance to prove that she belonged here, alongside so many great players. If she played badly, she knew that she might not get another opportunity.

Moments later, feeling a strange mixture of nerves and excitement, Chloe joined the rest of the squad as they made their way out onto the pitch. She was being thrown in at the deep end, starting the match, rather than just being subbed off the bench later in the game.

Then, as she lined up to shake the hands of the opposition players, she felt a sense of inner calm. She had spent her entire life training for this moment. Now, she knew she was ready.

The game kicked off, and straight away Chloe got stuck in, causing problems for the Watford defence.

She picked the ball up on the wing, dancing both left and right, drawing defenders away from her team-mates. This gave Arsenal far more space, enabling them slowly to get a grip on the play. It felt as if it would be only a matter of time before Arsenal scored.

Sure enough, just 16 minutes in, the ball fell to Leah Williamson in the box. Watford's defence failed to deal with it, and she fired past Trippoli Witney in goal.

GOAL! Arsenal had the lead.

Shaken by this early goal, Watford struggled to reset. They started making loose passes and were no longer getting tight to the Arsenal forwards.

Then, just six minutes later, Danielle Carter found herself in space on the wing. She received the ball and, without looking up, whipped it into the box.

Chloe sensed her opportunity. She was one step ahead of any of the Watford players in reacting to the flight of the ball, darting into the box and meeting the cross with a powerful header. The ball flew past the keeper and nestled in the back of the net.

GOAL!

For Chloe, the world suddenly seemed to stand still. She couldn't believe it! She had just scored her first goal in senior football – and she was still less than half an hour into her debut.

Now Arsenal were 2-0 up and cruising. Chloe had scored the goal that had really finished the match as a contest – there was no way back for Watford now.

After her goal, the rest of the game seemed to pass Chloe by in a blur. In the end, Arsenal ran out 3-0 winners.

Chloe had started, scored, and ended the match – all on her first day in senior football.

"Fantastic, Chloe!" Pedro said with a wide grin, as they walked back to the dressing room. "You've got everything it takes to succeed here. You're going to be a very important player for us!"

6
ON LOAN

June 2016, Select Security Stadium, Widnes, England
Continental Cup, Everton v Liverpool

"Welcome to Everton, Chloe." Andy Spence, Everton's manager, shook Chloe's hand enthusiastically.

"I'm happy to be here," Chloe replied with a grin. "I can't wait to get started."

After her strong Arsenal debut against Watford, Chloe had had a tough year at Arsenal. She felt she hadn't been able to meet her own expectations in subsequent games, and she'd found game-time hard to come by in a team filled with experienced superstars.

Even so, there had been some high points. In February, she'd signed with Arsenal in her first professional contract as a senior player – and she'd come off the bench to help secure a 5-1 win over Sunderland.

But she hadn't managed to cement herself as a regular starter.

At first, Chloe had been content with the fact that she was now a professional player but, in the end, it was her desire to be playing more regularly that had won out.

It had come to a head when she'd started on the bench in the Women's FA Cup final – in which Arsenal had beaten Chelsea 1-0. Chloe hadn't been called on in the game at all.

That had been a wake-up call. How could she develop as a player, and build a legacy for herself in professional football, if her team were winning critical games without her even being involved? Now Chloe knew – she had to find a way to gain more first-team experience, to fight her way back into Arsenal's starting eleven.

So now here she was, in Andy Spence's office, having just signed – on loan – for WSL2 club Everton.

As soon as she'd arrived, Chloe knew that she'd made the right decision. This was her opportunity to establish herself as one of the most exciting prospects in English football.

It was a change of club, but it was a change of home too. For the first time in her life, Chloe was now living away from her family and her friends in London. She knew that she'd probably end up feeling homesick at times, but it was a price she was prepared to pay.

Anyway, many top players spent their entire careers moving from club to club, even from country to country. She'd just have to learn to deal with.

Chloe's first game for Everton came in the Continental Cup, just as it had done for Arsenal. This time, it was against Everton's bitter local rivals, Liverpool. Chloe knew what the Merseyside derby meant to Everton fans, and she was determined to have an impact.

The game was cagey and physical, with both sides reluctant to commit forward and risk coming unstuck in defence. Chloe was playing well, in her now-traditional style, weaving in and out of defenders, playing passes to team-mates and causing chaos in the Liverpool ranks.

Then, on the stroke of half-time, the Everton plan was shaken by a goal from Liverpool's Emma Lundh. The goal had come at the worst possible time and, looking around, Chloe could see her team-mates' heads drop.

Everton's problems were made worse when their second-half substitute, Ellie Stewart, was sent off in the 71st minute, and the game ended in a 1-0 win for Liverpool.

Despite the loss, Chloe remained in good spirits. She knew that she'd played well, and it had only been a single goal. On another day, with a bit more luck, things might easily have been different.

"Great effort, Chloe," Andy said to her at full-time. "You played your socks off for 90 minutes there. Brilliant job!"

It never felt good being on the losing team, but Chloe was content to know she'd played her part well.

If she kept this up, she would establish herself as a key player for Everton – for sure.

7
WAITING FOR THE FUTURE

June 2017, Hanwell, London, England

As Chloe walked along the familiar streets to her parents' house, she thought about all that she'd accomplished over the past year.

She'd taken the bold step of going out on loan to Everton, moving to an unfamiliar city – and it had given her invaluable experience.

She had played in nine games for the club – often

playing for the full 90 minutes, rather than making the 15 or 20-minute substitute appearances that she was used to at Arsenal. She'd scored twice for Everton too.

At the end of the season, she had returned to Arsenal as an experienced senior player who'd proved to Everton, to Arsenal and to herself that she was a useful asset to any team.

But then, back at Arsenal, some of the old familiar problems had returned. She'd been given more game time, but had still struggled to really prove herself.

In just her second match back at Arsenal, Chloe had been in the starting eleven, but she'd failed to make an impact and had eventually been substituted for Danielle Carter, who'd scored twice and won the game.

After that, Chloe had started to have doubts about her quality. After all, Arsenal already had world-class players playing in her position – perhaps she just wasn't good enough.

The Arsenal manager, Pedro Martínez Losa, had tried to reassure her. "You're a talent for the future, Chloe," he'd told her. "As long as Danielle is here, it's going to be difficult for you to get regular game time.

But there will come a day when she moves on – and then, no doubt, you will be the star of the team."

This was reassuring to hear, but Chloe hadn't wanted to wait for the future to come to her. She'd wanted to be playing regular top-level football *now*.

It had been obvious that Arsenal hadn't wanted Chloe to leave but, if she'd been honest with herself, she hadn't been sure she'd wanted to stay.

Chloe was brought back to reality as she recognised the familiar street where, as a child, she'd played football between the bumps in the road. She was nearly home.

As she reached the house, her dad, Noel, opened the door for her.

"Come on in," he said, embracing his daughter.

It was good to see her family again, even if it was just to have lunch with them. Chloe's hectic professional commitments meant that, nowadays, there weren't many opportunities for the whole family to be together. Chloe always looked forward to it, as a welcome relief and a change of pace.

After lunch, discussion turned to Chloe's plans for her future in football. This was the first time since her new Arsenal contract that she'd had a chance to discuss it all with them properly.

"How was it at Everton anyway, Chloe?" Jamie asked. "That's a long way to go for a loan."

"Would you ever go back?" Paris added.

Chloe collected her thoughts before replying. "Yeah … I think I would go back," she said, suddenly feeling more sure of herself. "Right now, I think Everton is the best place for me to develop my football."

"Well, we'll support you wherever you go," Jane said. "And you'll always know where we are, if you need us."

Later that afternoon, when Chloe left her parents' home, she did so with a renewed sense of determination.

She wasn't going to wait around until Arsenal finally decided that she was ready. She would prove that she was ready now, by returning to Everton – again on loan.

Then, as luck would have it, a week later Chloe heard the news that Everton would be playing WSL football for the following season, after Notts County had disbanded.

So, next season, she'd still be playing regularly in the WSL after all. Just for Everton, rather than for Arsenal.

8
WELCOME HOME

October 2017, ARMCO Arena, Solihull, England
Women's Super League, Birmingham v Everton

"Are you settling back in OK?" Everton team-mate Simone Magill asked Chloe, as the players made their way towards the dressing room. "I remember when you first arrived here on loan. You were all nerves," Simone added with a laugh. "You're definitely different now!"

"It's good to be back. Everton feels like my home now," Chloe replied.

She remembered how she'd felt when she'd joined Everton the first time. Despite the change of club, she'd really still been concentrating on her future at Arsenal.

Now, things were different. This time, she was totally committed to Everton, fully focused on the job at hand.

Today was her second game back in the Toffees' colours. Her first had been a 2-0 loss to Liverpool – she'd started on the bench, being subbed on late in the game.

As the Everton players made their way towards the ARMCO Arena dressing room for today's game against Birmingham, they were all quietly wondering the same thing.

Will I be starting?

Chloe knew that she needed to establish herself as a key player in the team – and that meant getting regular starts.

"You'll be starting today, I'm sure of it," Simone told her, bringing Chloe back to reality. "We all saw how much you wanted it against Liverpool."

Desire was something that Chloe wasn't short of. She just needed to show that she could deliver – on the big stage, with a ball at her feet.

In the sparsely furnished away-team dressing room, the Everton manager, Andy Spence, called for the players' attention.

"We all know we have a difficult task ahead of us today," he began. "Birmingham recently made it to a Champions League semi-final, so they're no walkover."

A few murmurs could be heard amongst the players. Andy was right, this would be no easy game.

"If we're the underdogs – that's fine by us. It means the pressure's on them," Andy continued, hushing the chatter. "You'll need to be patient out of possession. They'll want to dominate the ball. We must be flexible and not get drawn into their trap," he said. "Today I want to try a 4-4-1-1 formation. Courtney, you will lead the line. Just behind will be Simone, with Marthe supporting on the left and Chloe on the right."

Andy continued through the team sheet, reading out the names and positions of the other players, but Chloe was barely listening. She had been given the news she was hoping for. She would be starting the match, alongside Courtney Sweetman-Kirk, Simone Magill and Marthe Munsterman in attack.

The game itself started just as Andy had predicted, with Birmingham dominating possession in the early exchanges. This was not going to be easy.

But this was a style of play that Chloe was now accustomed to. She was no longer the girl who had relentlessly chased down every ball in her early days at the QPR academy. She had learned so much about patient play since then, and now she was adept at counter-pressing.

Not everyone in the Everton ranks was quite so experienced, however, and just 14 minutes in, Ellen White broke through Everton's defensive lines, before smashing the ball past Elizabeth Durack and into the net.

Birmingham were 1-0 up.

Then, 31 minutes into the half, Chloe had to look on helplessly as Birmingham striker, Charlie Wellings, doubled their lead.

Everton managed to regain some composure, but at half-time they were still 2-0 down. The players knew that they had a mountain to climb to get back into the game.

Back in the dressing room, Andy tried to rally the team.

"We need to be using our wings more," he told the players. "Chloe and Marthe were making good runs out there, but we weren't finding them enough."

He made one change at half-time, substituting Marthe for Claudia Walker, putting some fresh legs on the left wing.

As Chloe made her way back out onto the pitch, she noticed that the Birmingham keeper, Ann-Katrin Berger, had been replaced by Frances Stenson. Chloe knew that substitute keepers sometimes made mistakes when they weren't quite up to speed in a match, so she made a mental note to shoot as early and as often as possible.

The referee's whistle blew for the start of the second half, and almost immediately Chloe got the chance she'd been waiting for.

The ball fell to her feet after ricocheting off the leg of a defender, and suddenly it was just Chloe against the onrushing keeper. Chloe took a small touch, then dinked the ball over Stenson and into the back of the net.

GOAL!

In the blink of an eye, the outlook of the game had changed. Chloe had had the impact she'd been looking for and, as the Everton players celebrated the goal, she could see the fire back in their eyes. They could see a way back into the game.

But, despite their best efforts, Everton couldn't break through again, and at the end of the match the score remained 2-1 to Birmingham.

Everton had lost by a narrow margin, but they had demonstrated their resolve. Most important for Chloe though, was the fact that she'd shown how much Everton needed her.

As the Everton players trooped off the pitch, Simone caught up to Chloe.

"How you played out there … " she said, still struggling for breath. "That was special. It's just like you never left. Welcome home!"

9
HAT-TRICK HEROINE

November 2017, Select Security Stadium, Widnes, England
Continental Cup, Everton v Oxford United

After just a few months back with Everton, Chloe had established herself as a regular starter for the club. Now she was one of the first names on Andy Spence's team sheet every week.

Tonight, Everton were playing in the Continental Cup against Oxford United, another team from a lower division.

Cup matches were famous for giant-killings, and Chloe wasn't going to take anything for granted.

Her confidence had increased enormously since returning to Everton, and she no longer worried about how much game time she was getting. Now her focus was on honing her skills and gaining valuable experience.

As the Everton players made their way out onto the pitch, Chloe caught up with Courtney Sweetman-Kirk.

"With the two of us in attack, Oxford won't know what's hit them," Chloe asserted confidently. "They don't stand a chance."

"Don't forget – they'll expect a challenge today," Courtney replied. "They'll be set up to defend. It won't be easy for us to find space."

Courtney was an experienced forward – and Chloe could see that she was right. She would need to choose her moments wisely. If she went out all guns blazing from the first minute, she wouldn't have the stamina to maintain a high level for the whole match. This game would be a marathon, not a sprint.

Chloe made a mental note to spend more time listening to wise heads like Courtney's. There was so much to learn about the finer points of winning games.

Out on the pitch, Chloe began her individual warm-up. This was usually the time when she played out various match scenarios in her mind – she saw herself drifting wide, cutting in from the wing and firing shot after shot at the Oxford keeper. It was her way of preparing mentally for a game.

Back in the dressing room, just before kick-off, Chloe could feel the tension in the room. Not all her team-mates were used to starting a match, and nerves were clearly beginning to creep in.

"Hey, everybody! Come on! If you weren't good enough to be playing today, the gaffer wouldn't be starting you," Chloe said with a warm smile. "We know what we have to do out there. We stay focused, we'll win this."

"How do you seem so confident, before a game like this?" one of the players asked Chloe.

"I just think that I'm the best," Chloe replied with a smile. "Don't get me wrong – it's not about being arrogant. It's just that, if you go out thinking that, then you'll play with much more freedom. It's about getting your head in the right place."

Chloe was still only 19 years old, but already she was starting to think like a seasoned veteran.

Her words helped raise the mood in the dressing room, and the players walked out onto the pitch feeling much more positive.

Chloe knew that Oxford would try to stay in the game for as long as possible, before making a late attempt to grab a winner. That was why she wanted to kill the game off early, by scoring first and then forcing Oxford to come out and play. That way, they'd be more vulnerable to attack.

Right from the off, Chloe sprang into action, closing down the Oxford defence and making it difficult for them to play at the slower pace they preferred. Everton's pressure was forcing the Oxford players into making mistakes, and they were struggling to find each other with accurate passes.

Just ten minutes in, the ball bounced toward an Oxford defender and, under pressure from Everton, the ball fell to Chloe. She sprinted through the defensive line and slotted the ball through the legs of the stranded Oxford keeper.

GOAL!

The Everton players ran to Chloe to celebrate the goal, but Chloe was already running straight back to her own half, keen to restart the match.

She knew that one goal wasn't enough to kill off the game. Everton needed more.

Despite the pressure, Oxford managed to hold on for the rest of the first half, and at half-time Everton led by Chloe's single goal.

In the dressing room, Andy only had words of encouragement for her. "Keep it up, Chloe. You're doing great. It's only a matter of time before Oxford cave in!"

He obviously saw things in the same way as Chloe.

The second half saw more of the same, with Everton pressing hard and dictating the game, and Oxford just about clinging on.

Chloe drove towards goal again and again, but with each attempt she was stopped at the last moment by a flailing Oxford tackle.

Oxford tried to stick to their game plan, and tried to score on the break at every opportunity. But Everton held firm.

Then, with just 20 minutes left, Claudia Walker found herself with a clear route to goal. The tired Oxford defence couldn't get back in to tackle her, and she calmly finished to double the Everton lead.

This second goal seemed to break the Oxford resolve. Chloe knew that, at 2-0 down and so late in the game, it was now close to impossible for them to come back. She decided to take full advantage of this.

Just nine minutes before the full 90, the chance Chloe had been waiting for finally arrived. An 18-yard box scramble led to an Oxford defender failing to clear her lines – and the ball fell straight to Chloe.

She took one touch, turned, and fired the ball into the top-right corner of the goal, past the desperate dive of the keeper.

GOAL!

She had just scored a brace, to give Everton an unassailable 3-0 lead over Oxford.

But Chloe wasn't done yet. Just two minutes later, Everton once again drove into the box, before an Oxford defender made a rash challenge which was completely mistimed. The ref pointed straight at the spot.

Nobody was surprised when Chloe picked up the ball to take the penalty. She had never felt so in control of a match before.

The referee's whistle sounded, and Chloe confidently strode up to the ball, blazing it down the centre of the goal. Despite the keeper getting a hand to it, she was powerless to prevent it finding the back of the net.

GOAL!

Chloe had just scored her first hat-trick in senior football. She had played the perfect game – and had swept Everton to victory.

The game ended 4-0 to Everton – an emphatic scoreline that sent a strong message to Everton's WSL opponents.

It was rare for a loan player to score a brace, let alone a hat-trick in a match. But now Chloe was sure that this loan couldn't go on for much longer. Surely, Everton couldn't ignore the chance to sign her permanently?

She was no longer just a useful member of the squad.

Now she was indispensable.

10
PERMANENT

February 2018, Select Security Stadium, Widnes, England
Women's Super League, Everton v Reading

"Still living off that hat-trick, eh?" Lizzie Durack, the Everton keeper, joked with Chloe.

"Of course I am! You're a keeper, Lizzie – what would *you* know about scoring goals?" Chloe grinned.

"I know how it feels to concede goals," Lizzie chuckled, "and if I was the Oxford keeper, I'd want to forget about that game as quickly as possible."

In the months after her famous hat-trick against Oxford, Chloe had been doing everything possible to cement her position at Everton – and to develop her skills and her understanding of game management.

And, just as she'd hoped – recognising her massive contribution to the club during her loan spells, in January the manager and the board had made the deal permanent.

Chloe was thrilled. It showed that all her hard work had been worth it. She was now at a club that fully appreciated her value – and wanted to put her at the centre of the team.

Signing permanently for Everton did finally close the door on the long and fruitful chapter of her life at Arsenal, though – and that was bittersweet. She was leaving behind friends and committing her career to the north of England, far from her home in London.

But Chloe knew that those kinds of changes were inevitable. She had promised herself that she'd become the best player she possibly could – and she couldn't have achieved that if she'd stayed at Arsenal.

Today's opponents were Reading, in the WSL.

The match was particularly important to the Everton players as, just two months ago, they'd been beaten by Reading in a penalty shootout in the Continental Cup.

In that game, Chloe had scored a dramatic late equaliser in extra time, to force penalties. But Everton had then lost their composure and missed two of their penalties, resulting in a 4-3 loss.

Today was their opportunity for revenge. The cup was one thing, but the league was far more important. A win today would demonstrate Everton's growing strength in the WSL.

Chloe had one other reason to prove her quality today. This was her first match at the Select Security Stadium since joining Everton permanently. She wanted to prove to the Everton fans that she was worthy of their number 11 shirt.

She also wanted to prove to herself, once and for all, that she had made the right decision. She wasn't just the girl from Hanwell anymore – now she was one of the most promising forwards in English football.

There had never been any doubt that Chloe could

score in front of goal. Everybody who watched her knew that she was a lethal finisher.

But recently, in her time at Everton, she'd been working hard to improve her playmaking skills. Now, she could drop deeper into midfield to pick the ball up, before driving towards the opposition defence and laying it off at the last second to a team-mate in space.

Finding that kind of killer pass to set up one of her team-mates just increased her versatility and her value to Everton.

"Play with freedom, Chloe," Andy told her, as she laced up her boots in the dressing room. "When you're on the ball, nobody knows what you'll do next – and that's one of your greatest strengths. Reading will find you a real handful."

"Thanks, boss. I'll do you proud out there."

As the players finished getting ready, Courtney Sweetman-Kirk beckoned Chloe over.

"Look for me out there – when you can," she said. "I'll be running off the last defender. As soon as you pick up the ball, I'll try to find space for you."

"I'll get you the ball – just make sure it ends up in the goal!" Chloe grinned.

If anyone knew how to find the back of the net, it was Courtney. Together, she and Chloe made a formidable partnership up front for Everton – and Chloe was aware that, often, it was Courtney assisting her.

Chloe could hear the thrum of the crowd growing louder as kick-off grew nearer. She began to make her way out onto the pitch with the rest of the team.

Her days of waiting on the bench for a substitute appearance that might never come were now long gone.

The game got underway, and the early exchanges were fiercely contested. Both sides were eager to stamp their authority on the game, and Chloe realised that this could easily slip out of Everton's hands – as it had done so cruelly in the Continental Cup. She was determined that, this time, it wouldn't happen.

Just six minutes in, as the Reading defenders were still finding their footing in the game, Chloe seized her opportunity.

She picked the ball up on the right wing and sprinted past the defensive midfielder, before looping a ball into the centre of the box, where she knew Courtney would be waiting. Chloe didn't even need to look up.

The cross was sweetly struck, and it landed right at Courtney's feet, giving her an easy finish, which she calmly dispatched.

Everton had the lead.

"That didn't take long," Chloe said triumphantly, over the cheers of the crowd.

"With passing like that, how could I possibly miss?" Courtney replied enthusiastically. "Now it's your turn to get on the scoresheet," she added.

Chloe had surprised even herself at the speed with which Everton had broken the deadlock. In December, they'd taken 112 minutes to beat the Reading defence – today it had only taken six.

With the wind in their sails, Everton pushed on to kill the game off as quickly as possible.

Under mounting pressure, Reading continued holding firm, until Chloe found herself with some space to work with.

She drove at the Reading left-back, drawing her in, before the defence scrambled. Then, in trying to tackle her, they left Chloe with just the Reading keeper, Mary Earps, to beat.

By now, one-on-one situations were second nature to Chloe, and she casually finished, slotting the ball into the bottom-left corner.

GOAL!

Chloe had given Everton the two-goal cushion they needed to feel more comfortable in the game. In just 23 minutes, she had a goal and an assist under her belt.

At half-time, the score was 2-1 to Everton, after Rachel Furness pulled one back just before half-time. But even so, Everton were the dominant side.

"What a pass," Courtney said, as they walked into the dressing room. "Not long ago, you'd never have found me there. It's like you've gained a sixth sense for passing."

Courtney was exaggerating, but Chloe knew what she meant. Earlier in her career, Chloe had been focused solely on her own performance, just thinking about scoring the next goal. Now she was far more composed – she could see the bigger picture within a match.

The second half began in cagey fashion. Reading knew they only needed one goal to get a result, so were hesitant to go all out for the win. This meant that they spent much of the second half chasing Everton players, rather than attacking the Everton defence.

Then, just on 90 minutes, Andy gestured to the fourth official that he wanted to make a sub. Chloe was momentarily confused, as substitutions this late were usually only made by a team that was defending for their lives. And here, Everton were quite comfortable.

Then Chloe saw her number 11 raised on the board and she understood, The Everton manager was substituting her, so she could soak in the applause from the Everton fans for her performance.

As she slowly made her way off the pitch, Chloe allowed herself a moment to take in the applause, and to appreciate all she'd achieved so far.

She'd come to Everton in 2016 – on loan – a shy girl from Hanwell, without much confidence.

Now, she was a permanent Everton player, with a killer instinct, boundless confidence – and the love of the Everton fans.

She was on top of the world.

II
EMPHATIC

August 2018, Stade de Marville, Saint-Malo, France
U20 World Cup, England U20 v Mexico U20

"Right! Listen up, everybody! I want you to focus on the positives today," the England Under-20s manager, Mo Marley, told them, as the players stood in the dressing room after their warm-up. "We all know our life is on the line here – but see it as an opportunity to get to the next stage, rather than something to be nervous about."

England had started the Under-20s World Cup in

strong form. With so many WSL players in their ranks, they were expected to go far.

They'd started impressively, beating North Korea 3-1 in the opening match.

But then, in the following game against Brazil, they'd shown their vulnerability. England had taken the lead in the eleventh minute – from a Georgia Stanway penalty – and had been in control, until victory was taken away in the dying embers by a stoppage-time equaliser from Brazil's Ariadina.

That draw meant that England were now going into their third group match, today's game against Mexico, on four points. A win would put them in the knockout stages. A loss would send them home.

Mo Marley was right – their life was on the line.

Chloe had played in both of the first two games, but hadn't yet managed to score – something she was determined to change today. Especially as today's game was easily the most important of her international career so far.

In the dressing room, Mo Marley was continuing her pep-talk with the players. She was interrupted by

Chloe Peplow, who voiced what many of the players were thinking.

"What if we go behind?" she asked.

"The plan doesn't change," Mo replied quickly. "If they do take the lead, they will change their plan. They will try to hold on to what they have, and will invite pressure. The game is never lost when we're only one goal down. Come the final whistle, you'll finish winners."

The confidence of their manager seemed to calm the players, and Chloe could sense that her team-mates were now all on the same page. They were ready.

As part of the team's preparations, Chloe had taken the time to study the Mexico players she would be up against in the game.

This was yet another way of improving her game that Chloe had found. It meant that she could work out the weaknesses in the opposition and find the best way to exploit them – all before a ball had even been kicked.

Today, she would be playing off the left-hand side of the attack, meaning that she'd mostly be dealing with the Mexico right-midfielder, Montserrat Hernández, and right-back, Ashley Lauren Soto.

They were both quick to the ball, but Chloe had seen that, if she could lure them into a tackle, she would be able to turn at the last second and pass them.

She'd only need one chance.

Right from the kick-off, the nervousness of both sides was clear to see. Passes weren't quite as crisp as usual, and both teams were unable to create chances.

The game looked as if it was getting bogged down in stalemate, but then suddenly the ball bounced free of the clutches of the Mexico midfield, and Chloe was the first to it.

Before she had a chance to set herself, however, Hernández was on her in a flash. Chloe realised that she would have to be much quicker if she was going to beat her marker in this game.

With time ticking down towards half-time, the first goal finally came – but it wasn't for England. Thirty-seven minutes in, Lizbeth Ovalle found the space to shoot – and fired Mexico into a 1-0 lead.

The half-time whistle came as a relief to the England players, who'd clearly been rattled by the Mexico goal and were in danger of conceding a second.

As the players caught their breath in the dressing room, Chloe walked over to Lauren Hemp, who was playing in the centre of England's attack. Chloe was sure that, if she could draw defenders in to her, then Lauren would have more space to work with, and might have more opportunities to score.

"If you wait for me to receive the ball, I can draw the Mexico players away from you," Chloe said to Lauren. "Then you'll be able to get a clear sight of goal."

"Good idea, Chloe," Lauren replied with a grin. "They were all over me in the first half – I could use all the space you can get me."

Understanding the big picture before a game was always very important. This was the manager's job, but sometimes only the players could pick up on subtle changes during a game – changes that could make a huge difference on the pitch.

As the second half began, Chloe could sense that Mexico were looking confident. But their 1-0 lead was a slender one, and she felt sure that they wouldn't be able to protect it for long.

Just four minutes into the second half, Chloe drifted

out wide, drawing the Mexico players on the right-hand side towards the touchline. Just as Chloe had suggested, this gave Lauren all the space she needed deftly to head the ball for Alessia Russo, who equalised.

It was 1-1. Game on.

The wind was behind England now, and they continued to keep up the pressure, maintaining a relentless pace.

In the 53rd minute, Chloe got the chance she'd been waiting for.

Sandy MacIver sent the ball long from her goal kick, and the ball fell just short of Chloe, who deftly feinted towards the ball, before allowing it to run past her. This split the Mexico defence and left her one-on-one with the Mexico keeper.

Before Mexico knew what had hit them, Chloe expertly finished into the bottom left corner of the goal.

2-1. Now England were firing on all cylinders.

Chloe's goal broke the spirit of the Mexico team. In just eight minutes in the second-half, Mexico had seen their one-goal lead crumble. Now they found themselves trailing.

The furious England attacks continued to besiege the Mexico defence for the rest of the match.

In the end, England won the game 6-1, with Chloe also registering two assists.

England had not just won the game emphatically – they had also guaranteed progression to the World Cup knockout stages, showing that they were not a team to be taken lightly.

On a personal level, Chloe had demonstrated that she was now the ultimate forward. She could run, pass and shoot with devastating accuracy – and she had an excellent understanding of the game.

And she was still only 20 years old – with a long career ahead of her.

The only way was up.

12
SIDELINED

February 2019, Finch Farm, Halewood, England

"Hey, Chloe! How are you holding up?" Willie Kirk, the new Everton manager, asked, walking over to where Chloe was standing.

"Not too bad thanks, gaffer. I miss playing football already, though," Chloe replied, managing to put on a smile, despite her frustration.

"Well, this surgery is the best thing for you in the

long-term. Take your time to recover properly now and you'll be back – and better than ever – in no time," Willie answered, managing a somewhat unconvincing smile.

"You're right – I was only making it worse by playing on. I'll do my best to be fully fit in time for next season, boss."

It had been less than a week since Chloe's ankle surgery, and already she was desperate to be back in football.

Following the Young Lionesses' dominant display against Mexico, the Under-20s World Cup had not gone the way Chloe had hoped.

A 2-0 semi-final defeat to eventual winners Japan had ended England's chance of winning the tournament, although a penalty shootout victory in the third-place decider had meant that Chloe had returned home with the bronze medal.

Chloe was pleased with her progress – this was the most success she'd had with the national team, but of course she'd wanted Gold.

Then, before the start of the 2018-19 WSL season,

Chloe had picked up an innocuous ankle injury in training.

She'd thought nothing of it at the time – footballers were getting knocks and scrapes all the time, and her days in the cages with her brothers had prepared her for that. So she'd kept it quiet at first, preferring to try to play through the pain.

But, after a while, Chloe could tell that this was different. The injury was severely impacting her form and, with just one goal all season, she'd finally decided to do something about it.

The result was that she'd needed ankle surgery – and now, with just seven games remaining in the season, she was going to be out of action for all of them.

This was something Chloe hadn't faced before in her career. In the injury-prone world of women's football, she'd been fortunate to avoid anything significant – until now.

But even with the injury, Chloe didn't want to be away from football. At a time when most injured players would be at home recovering, she continued attending training, to watch the players and to keep up with tactics.

Today she was watching an attack v defence drill on the training pitch. Being on the side-lines with the coaching staff, rather than being on the pitch, gave Chloe a different view of the game.

She marvelled at the fluidity of the forward play. It was true that Everton were struggling in the league, but that was clearly more about the quality of the other WSL teams, than about any weaknesses at Everton.

She saw the movement of the attackers and knew where the next pass should go. In her mind's eye, she kicked every ball, desperate to be involved.

Chloe was glad to have already established herself as an essential player for Everton. She'd heard stories of more marginal players who'd faced a long recovery from injury, and had never been the same player again.

Just then, as the players finished the drill and took a breather, Inessa Kaagman wandered over to Chloe.

"I bet it's killing you not being able to play, right?" Inessa asked.

Inessa was another of Everton's forwards and, no doubt, the Dutch winger would be getting more game time as a result of Chloe being injured. Nevertheless, everyone in women's football understood that any injury was a serious business, and Inessa wanted to make sure Chloe was managing it.

"It is," Chloe answered glumly. "I feel like I'm missing so much already, and it's only been a week. Months of this is going to feel like torture!"

"I know," Inessa said, sounding serious. "Recovery is all about taking it a day at a time. You can't rush your return, or you'll do yourself more damage in the long run. Trust me – I should know. I've got a medicine degree!" she added with a grin.

"Thanks, Inessa. Do me proud out there – I'll be watching," Chloe said encouragingly.

As frustrating as the injury was, Chloe knew that, in the scheme of things, it would prove to be just a minor hiccup in her career. One day she would be able to look back and see it in perspective. She might even be able to say that she'd learned something from it.

But, in the meantime, Chloe just wanted to get back to playing football as quickly as possible.

13
REJUVENATED

September 2019, Haig Avenue, Southport, England
Women's Super League, Everton v Bristol City

"How's the ankle feeling?" Inessa asked Chloe, bringing her back to reality.

"Better than ever," Chloe replied enthusiastically. "I just want to get out there and show everyone what they've been missing."

This was Everton's first home match of the new season, and Chloe wanted to put on a show for the Haig

Avenue crowd. Chloe hadn't played much at Everton's temporary new home before, as they'd moved there shortly before her injury.

Just then, somebody opened the dressing room door, and the noise of the crowd was suddenly shockingly loud.

"Can you hear that out there? They'll all be cheering your name," Inessa said, reading Chloe's thoughts. "With us on the wings, they'll have a lot to be excited about."

With just moments to go before kick-off, Willie Kirk came over to Chloe. "I can't tell you how good it is to see you back in the team, Chloe," he said.

"Thanks, boss. It feels great to be back. This season's going to be a good one," she declared. "I just know it."

"I wouldn't want to be on the other team when you're this fired up," he chuckled.

Willie Kirk had a point. Having made a full recovery from her ankle surgery, today Chloe wanted nothing more than to demonstrate exactly what she could do.

As the players lined up in the tunnel, Chloe allowed herself a moment to reflect on her career. The young girl from Ealing who had dreamed of making something of herself in football was long gone.

Now she was a well-established, top-level WSL player. She'd won bronze at the Under-20s World Cup, and had made her England senior debut in a friendly against Austria. Now she had her sights firmly fixed on becoming a regular for England and – more immediately – becoming a dominant force for Everton.

Chloe walked with the team out onto the pitch and lined up to shake hands with the Bristol City players. They were giving her sideways glances, and she could tell that they knew she was one of Everton's dangerous players. Her reputation as a matchwinner had preceded her – and today she was going to make sure that the Bristol City players understood why.

As the game got underway, Chloe wasted no time before making her presence felt.

During her time on the side-lines, Chloe had noticed some issues in the way that the Everton forwards coordinated a press against the opposition defenders.

They would often press one by one, which occasionally worked if the defender made a mistake, but all-too-often the press could be bypassed with a simple pass.

Since returning to playing, Chloe had been working

hard with the other Everton forwards to press much more as a unit.

The early stages of the game were evidence that this work was beginning to pay off. Simone Magill, in the centre of the pitch, would pressure the Bristol City centre-back when they were on the ball, and then, when they passed to the left or right, Chloe or Inessa would support her and close off the passing lanes.

Bristol City dominated possession for much of the first half, but Everton's systematic press made sure that the stalemate was maintained and the away team were prevented from mounting their own attacks.

As half-time approached, Chloe got her chance. The Everton press won the ball, and Simone fed it into Chloe. She took one touch, before looking up and lacing it from outside of the box onto the left post – and into the back of the net.

The crowd erupted in celebration. This was the best goal they'd seen so far at Haig Avenue – and one of the best of Chloe's career.

"Now *that* is how to finish," Inessa shouted above the noise, embracing Chloe as they celebrated the goal.

"I've had a lot of time away to think about it," Chloe grinned.

Immediately after the restart, Chloe was onto the defence in a flash. The Bristol City players struggled to find a way out, and the ball fell to Molly Pike. She fizzed it into Chloe's feet, before Chloe blazed another shot from outside the box into the top-right corner of the goal.

In just two minutes, Everton had gone from a stalemate, at 0-0, to take a dominant 2-0 lead.

The crowd were beside themselves. They'd just been treated to two of the best goals they were ever likely to see – and Chloe had scored both of them.

"You're starting to make us look bad," Simone laughed, high-fiving Chloe. "Leave some goals for the rest of us."

"That was magnificent, Chloe," Willie Kirk told her at half-time. "Your ankle injury seems to have turned you into a superhuman!"

In some ways it was true. Somehow, Chloe had used her time away from playing to help her come back stronger than ever – both physically and mentally.

As the second half began, Chloe sensed that the fight seemed to have gone out of the Bristol City players. They were no longer playing with the same anxious energy that comes in a game you think you can win. They seemed to know that the game was already over.

And so it proved, as the final few minutes drained away and Chloe's team ran out 2-0 winners.

The job had been well-and-truly completed in two whirlwind first-half minutes.

Everton had won the first two games of the 2019-20 WSL season, and had shown the league that they were here to play – and were serious about it.

Chloe had worked through her injury scare and now she was back, making a real difference to the team.

She was back alright – and she was better than ever.

14
SCINTILLATING FORM

January 2020, Select Security Stadium, Widnes, England
Women's Super League, Everton v Reading

Following her recovery from injury, Chloe had gone from strength to strength. Since the brace against Bristol City, she'd scored three more goals and was coming into today's match, against Reading, in scintillating form.

Everton had gone from strength to strength too – largely on account of Chloe's talents.

They'd finished second-last in the previous campaign,

but this year they were giving the big teams a real headache.

Today's opponents, Reading, were one such team. They'd finished in the top five for the last three seasons, and were just the kind of club that Everton wanted to emulate.

Just before kick-off, Chloe took a walk around the Select Security Stadium. Everton were back at their old stomping ground for one final time, before their new ground, Walton Hall Park, would be open.

Chloe thought about all the good times – and the bad – that she'd experienced at Everton. Even the painful memories, such as her initial homesickness and her recent injury, had been important in making her the person she was today.

But she couldn't escape the niggling feeling she'd had in her final days with QPR – and then with Arsenal. Was it time to move? And, if so, where did she go from here?

There was no doubting that Everton had come on leaps and bounds, but Chloe wondered whether she'd reached her limit with the club. To become indispensable

– to her club *and* her country, might mean looking for new opportunities elsewhere. She knew she had to be on the radar of other clubs – she'd won WSL player of the month in September, and had been called up to the England squad again.

But that could all wait. Today was matchday, so Chloe turned her attention to the task at hand.

"Boo!" The voice of Danielle Turner, Everton's left-back, startled Chloe, bringing her back into the moment.

"Hey, are you trying to give me a heart attack or something?" Chloe laughed.

"Just keeping you on your toes," Danielle said. "You're going to need to be sharp against this lot."

"Don't tell me you've forgotten about the masterclass I put on against Reading in 2018!" Chloe teased.

"I remember, and I'm sure they haven't forgotten," Danielle laughed, knowing that Reading would have put a lot of thought into how to keep Chloe out of the game today.

Back in the dressing room, Chloe could feel the tension in the air. Was it because it was their final game at the Select Security Stadium, or was it because Everton had history against Reading?

Willie Kirk called the team over to talk through their game plan. Everton would be playing a 4-2-3-1 formation, with Chloe on the left wing and Danielle behind her at left-back.

This setup was second nature to Chloe now, and she seemed to have a sixth sense for where her team-mates would be on the pitch.

Out on the pitch, as they prepared to kick off, Chloe took a moment to watch the Reading right-back, Rachel Rowe. She was the defender Chloe would have the most contact with during the game. Would Chloe be able to find a weakness there?

Either way, she knew that Reading were an experienced side, with a number of internationals in their ranks. This would be no blowout.

Reading showed their mettle early on, with their forwards testing the Everton goal. But they met stubborn resistance from the Everton keeper, Sandy MacIver.

Then, just 11 minutes in – and seemingly out of the blue – the Everton winger, Chantelle Boye-Hlorkah, managed to scramble the ball into the box and across to where Chloe was positioned.

Chloe took no time in dispatching the ball into the bottom-right corner of the net. GOAL!

Against the run of play, Everton had the lead – and, to nobody's surprise, it was Chloe who'd found the net.

"They're scared to get close to you," Chantelle remarked, in the aftermath of the goal celebrations.

"I'd better make sure I keep giving them reasons to be scared, then," Chloe laughed.

But, after the restart, Reading showed just why they were such a strong force in the WSL. After besieging the Everton goal for 20 minutes, they finally found their equaliser.

Megan Finnigan was forced into a last-ditch tackle in the Everton box, and mistimed it. The resulting penalty was slotted away by Fara Williams.

It was 1-1 – and the tide seemed to be turning in Reading's favour.

Everton held firm for the remainder of the first half, and it was still level as the players made their way to the dressing room.

"We're living dangerously here. We need to tighten up in the second half," Willie told the Everton players.

"Yeah – they're finding too much space. At the rate it's going, they could score two or three, and take the game out of sight," Gabrielle George, the Everton centre-back, added.

"Right, I want the midfield to drop deeper and close down the space," Willie said firmly. "We'll have less in attack, but we can use the wings to create counter-attacks."

This suited Chloe. If Everton switched into a fast build-up, the Reading defenders would have less time to react – and Chloe would be able to find more space.

As the second half got underway, Everton's change in strategy seemed to be paying off. Though they were creating less, they were far more solid out of possession, and the momentum Reading had been building seemed to have been neutralised.

Then, with two-thirds of the game gone, Everton found an unlikely breakthrough.

Chloe had a corner on the left side of the pitch. She sent it in with a vicious bend, making sure to angle it towards the goal – and, for once, nobody got to it. The ball arced dangerously towards the far post and the Reading defenders all failed to get a head to it.

That left the keeper with no time to react, and the ball floated all the way into the net.

2-1. Everton had the lead again, in the strangest of ways.

"These poor Reading players aren't safe from you even when you're taking corners," Chantelle laughed.

This freak goal seemed to knock the stuffing out of Reading, and gradually the Everton players were able to wrestle back control of the game.

Then Chloe finished the game for good. Lucy Graham whipped the ball in from the left, and Chloe got onto it, slamming it home from close range to give Everton a 3-1 lead.

Chloe had a magnificent hat-trick.

"That's the first Everton hat-trick in the league for seven years," Lucy said, excitedly.

"I had a feeling this was going to be a special game," Chloe replied, laughing.

If the second goal hadn't finished the game,

Chloe's third certainly did. Reading seemed to consign themselves to defeat, hardly threatening the Everton goal for the rest of the match.

At full-time, Everton had beaten their close rivals 3-1, and Chloe had signed off at the Select Security Stadium with a magnificent hat-trick. It was her second hat-trick for Everton, and her first in the WSL.

Chloe was at the peak of her Everton career, and once again she began to think about whether her time at the club was coming to an end.

She had become Everton's hottest prospect and, no doubt, could have the pick of the bunch in choosing a new club. With her contract expiring in June, Chloe wondered whether now really was the time to make her move – to a club that could offer her the opportunity of European football.

She could already feel the adrenaline, just thinking about the prospect.

15
THE FUTURE IS BRIGHT

October 2020, Academy Stadium, Manchester, England
Women's Super League, Man City v Spurs

"Chloe! I'm open," Ellen White shouted, as she made a surging run through the centre of the Tottenham defence.

Without hesitation, Chloe lofted the ball over Kerys Harrop's head and into Ellen's path, before a last-ditch tackle from the Spurs centre-back stopped City from taking the lead.

Chloe was still getting used to the unfamiliar surroundings of the Academy Stadium in Manchester, but one thing that was unchanged was the threat she posed, running down the left wing.

At the end of the 2019-20 WSL season, Chloe had made the difficult decision to sign for Manchester City on a two-year contract.

She'd loved her time at Everton, but she had become a big fish in a small(ish) pond. If she was going to develop as a player, she needed to be stretched, challenged.

She needed to feel as if she was almost out of her depth.

Everton had wanted her to stay – of course – but Chloe knew that she owed it to herself to do what she thought was right for her career.

Manchester City were one of the strongest sides in English football. They had won the WSL in 2016, and had also finished runners-up in the COVID-shortened 2019-20 WSL season, meaning that this year they would be playing in the Champions League.

At City, Chloe would have the chance to establish herself in a top team – and hopefully push for contention in England's squad for Euro 2022, whilst playing with some of the best players in the world, and against some of the toughest opposition.

With the Euros almost two years away, Chloe now needed to show everyone why City had been so desperate to sign her. And today's game against Spurs gave her the opportunity to do just that.

Right from the kick-off, Chloe could sense that the Spurs defenders were wary of her. They obviously knew her from the reputation she'd acquired at Everton.

Chloe was playing in her familiar position on the left side of attack, alongside England legend Ellen White in the centre and Janine Beckie on the right.

This was a fearsome attacking unit.

"Keep it up, Chloe! They can't handle you," the City manager, Gareth Taylor, shouted from the side-lines.

There were just 20 minutes on the clock, but Spurs were already looking shaky. Surely it was only a matter of time before City would break the deadlock.

Relentlessly, Chloe drove down the left wing, picking the ball up in midfield and running straight at the Spurs defence, causing them to backpedal.

Then, suddenly, Chloe stopped the ball dead, before playing a powerful backwards pass to Stephanie Houghton, who was roaming forward. In turn, Stephanie found Ellen White, who fizzed a dangerous shot onto the Spurs crossbar.

With every attack, City were getting closer to scoring. It was a matter of *when*, not *if*, they would take the lead.

On 33 minutes, Chloe got the chance she'd been waiting for. Ellen drew a foul in the attacking third and, from the resulting free kick, Keira Walsh found Chloe.

From just outside the Spurs penalty area, Chloe looked up and fizzed a low shot into the bottom right corner of the Spurs goal.

GOAL!

"Now *that* is how to shoot," Ellen laughed, as the players celebrated the goal.

"I can teach you in training if you want," Chloe teased.

It was Chloe's first goal for her new club – and, with it, she had given City the lead.

Chloe knew that the stands would have been rocking

with celebrating City fans – if there had been any in attendance. But the COVID-19 pandemic was still affecting everything, and the regulations meant that fans were still prohibited from attending matches.

Even so, Chloe was sure that the City fans would be cheering, watching the game at home on TV.

The rest of the first half was largely uneventful, although two Spurs players were booked for bad fouls. Spurs were struggling to contain City, and were beginning to fall apart under increasing pressure.

Shortly after half-time, it was clear that Spurs hadn't worked out a way to deal with the City attack. Gemma Bonner was hacked down by a Spurs defender inside the box, which meant only one thing – penalty.

Despite being new to the club, Chloe's penalty-taking prowess was known to everyone in the WSL, and so it fell to her to take it.

Chloe calmly walked up to the spot. She'd noticed that the Spurs keeper was uncomfortable with penalties and would try to see where the penalty-taker was looking, before deciding on where to dive.

So Chloe kept her gaze dead-centre, before placing

the penalty into the bottom-left corner, beyond the stranded keeper.

With 40 minutes left to play, City were 2-0 up and – not for the first time in a match – Chloe had scored both of them. She was living up to her reputation as a match-winner.

Moments later, Sam Mewis added a third for City. The match was over as a contest, and Spurs set about trying to limit their losses, closing ranks and sitting in.

As a result, Chloe's impact on the wing was reduced. She was substituted shortly after, being replaced by Jessica Park.

Chloe's race was run. In little more than an hour, she'd shown, not just the City fans but the entire world, exactly what she had to offer.

She was now at the top of her game. The Champions League beckoned – as did the certain knowledge that she'd be playing for her country.

Chloe's future had never looked brighter.

16
ACL

November 2021, Etihad Stadium, Manchester, England

ACL.

Hearing those three letters was every footballer's worst nightmare. The mere thought of it was enough to send shivers down the spine. Because ACL was usually only talked about in terms of an injury.

The anterior cruciate ligament, or ACL, is one of the main ligaments in the knee – and damaging it is one of the worst injuries a football player can suffer. Sometimes it will end a career.

And, as bad luck would have it, in a routine WSL match against Birmingham in May, Chloe would find out first-hand just how bad it could be.

There had been just two games remaining in the 2020-21 WSL season, and City had been sitting in second place, due in large part to the quality of Chloe's play throughout the season.

Then disaster had struck.

Chloe had been on top form in the Birmingham game. She'd already scored two goals and looked as if she might get another, when she'd suffered a clash of knees with the Birmingham defender, Rebecca Holloway.

The clash had given City a penalty – but it hadn't been one that Chloe would be taking.

In a haze of pain, she'd been stretchered off, knowing straight away what the problem was – and knowing from her previous ankle injury that, at the very least, her season was at an end.

That had been six months ago. Now, despite the very real threat that an ACL injury posed to a player's career, Chloe knew that she was well on the way to a return to football.

Chloe was sitting on a Wattbike, in the gym at the Etihad campus. She was hard at work, following a structured recovery routine.

"How's it feeling today?" Lucy Bronze asked her. Lucy was also working on recovering from an injury she'd suffered.

"It's small steps," Chloe replied with a laugh. "Each day is better than the last, so I'm heading in the right direction!"

Making light of her situation had been important in keeping her focused on recovering, rather than dwelling on her injury.

"I remember how I felt during my recovery," Lucy added. She'd suffered a serious knee injury herself, early in her career, and knew how hard these kinds of injuries were to deal with. "You're doing great, Chloe – just keep focused on getting back into football, not on what you've missed."

This was something that the club doctor, Phil Clelland, had also recommended.

"Right now, Chloe, it probably feels like the end of the road for your career," he'd told her, in the days after her injury. "But I promise it isn't. We'll get you on a strict rehab programme and, if you stick to it – barring bad luck – you'll be back terrorising defences in no time."

His words had been a source of encouragement but, even so, the road to recovery was going to be a long one.

She'd had knee surgery just eight days after the injury – and it had been a success. But it was the rehabilitation that was going to be the most difficult for her. She'd known that it would probably be harder mentally than physically.

In those early days, Chloe had drawn on the support of her family. They'd helped her stay positive and prepare her for the path to recovery.

She'd known that if everything went perfectly – and if she got lucky – she might make a return to training in six months' time. But, more realistically, it might be a year away.

And with the Tokyo Olympics starting just two months after her injury, she'd known that she would miss out on representing Team GB there. This had been a real disappointment, as she'd known that she'd have been selected if she'd been fit.

So Chloe had decided to set her sights on returning in time to help City before the end of the 2021-22 WSL season. Plus, she'd do everything she could to get back in time to be selected for the 2022 Euros in July.

Now Chloe was six months into her recovery programme, and the doctors had told her that she was on track for a probable return in April 2022 – 11 months after her injury.

"At least, with every day that goes by, I'm getting closer to playing again," Chloe said to Lucy.

"Right. Focus on the positives. With any luck you'll be back in plenty of time to make it into the England squad. They won't have forgotten how good you are, just because you've been out for a while."

Lucy was right. Shortly after her injury, Chloe had been named the Man City Player of the Season, and she'd been shortlisted for the WSL Team of the Season. She wasn't going to be forgotten.

"Well, as long as I haven't lost all of my ability when I'm finally fit again," Chloe grinned nervously.

"No chance," Lucy smiled. "Besides, if you're even half as good as you were last season, Sarina Wiegman will have no choice but to include you in her Euros squad."

"Fancy some boxing?" Chloe asked, changing the subject.

"Sure! But you know – if there's one thing I'm better than you at, it's boxing," Lucy teased.

And so, Chloe's rehab continued. Hours spent in the gym, stretches, meetings with doctors and physios ... as well as training with Lucy on the bike and in the ring. Chloe couldn't wait to be back in football.

She'd suffered an injury many players would never recover from – but now she knew that it had its positives. She would come out of it mentally stronger – and even more determined to get straight back to the very top of professional football.

17
BACK IN STYLE

May 2022, Academy Stadium, Manchester, England
Women's Super League, Manchester City v Birmingham City

Chloe still wasn't used to this – sitting on the bench and watching the match kick off in front of her.

But that was the nature of returning from a long injury. Gareth Taylor, the City manager, had been carefully rationing her minutes, to ease her back into the game without risking any additional injury.

She'd finished rehab in April, 11 months after the

injury, but so far Chloe hadn't played a full 90 minutes in the WSL – and she hadn't managed to score. But there had been promising signs, including an assist in City's 4-0 win against Leicester.

She had, however, played the full 90 minutes in City's 4-1 victory over West Ham in the FA Cup semi-final, where she'd also scored a goal. That had set City up for the final, against Chelsea, in 11 days' time.

Chloe was desperate to get game time, especially against today's opponents, Birmingham – the team they'd been playing when she'd suffered her injury.

She felt fully fit, but she knew that the manager and physios were right to be careful. After all, Sarina Wiegman would be naming her provisional Euros squad in just two weeks. Another injury would give her no chance of England selection.

In her absence, City had largely continued their good form. They'd won the League Cup in March, beating Chelsea 3-1, but had been eliminated from the Champions League in the qualifying stages by Real Madrid. In the WSL, City hadn't quite reached the top.

In matches against teams lower in the table, City

were usually able to manage the game well. They had quality in depth and could usually find the winning goal.

But today's match was different. Birmingham were fighting for their lives on the brink of relegation and, desperate for the points, would fight City all the way.

Chloe watched the game from the bench, as the match bogged down in a defensive standoff. Neither side were making much progress, and Chloe's urge to get on grew with every scuffed shot and misplaced pass.

The Birmingham defenders scrambled whenever a City player came towards their goal, with last-ditch tackles flying in and players throwing themselves in the way of shots.

It wasn't elegant, but it was effective. Their stubborn resistance was blunting the City attack, and Chloe could see that her team were running out of ideas.

"Looks like we might be needed after all," Ellen White, sitting next to Chloe on the bench, told her.

"I can't stand all this waiting around," Chloe answered. "We could turn this game upside down if we were out there."

"The gaffer will come to the same conclusion soon

enough. But he'll want to leave it until the last possible minute – everyone's afraid that you'll do too much too soon and get injured again," Ellen added.

Chloe knew that Ellen was right. After an ACL injury, patience was absolutely essential. To injure her knee again would set Chloe back at least a year – which might mean missing the World Cup in 2023, as well as the Euros.

The stalemate continued for the rest of the first half. Then, as the players walked back to the dressing room at half-time, Gareth Taylor pulled Chloe aside.

"How are you feeling, Chloe?"

"I'm feeling good, gaffer – I just want to be out on the pitch," Chloe replied.

"The coaches think we'll need half-time substitutes today. Do you think you're ready?"

"I'm ready."

As City made their way out onto the pitch for the second half, the fourth official signalled City's half-time substitution. Hayley Raso off, Chloe Kelly on. She had 45 minutes to turn the game in City's favour.

Chloe took up her position on the right wing. By

now, she'd grown into the complete forward, and could play equally well on both sides of the pitch, using either foot. That kind of versatility always kept the defenders guessing.

Chloe made her presence felt almost immediately. Just three minutes in, she leapt above the Birmingham defence to meet Caroline Weir's corner, heading narrowly wide.

Birmingham were on the ropes and, with Chloe now on the pitch, City were able to keep the pressure up on the Blues' backline. Wave after wave of City attacks were being scrambled away at the last moment. The first City goal felt inevitable.

It came on 58 minutes. Keira Walsh picked the ball up in the middle of the pitch and drove towards goal. Timing her run perfectly, Chloe broke through the defence, drawing the Birmingham left-back and the left centre-back with her.

This gave City all the space they needed. Keira found Georgia Stanway with a deft pass, before she then laced a shot from the edge of the box into the bottom-left corner, beyond the outstretched glove of the keeper.

It was 1-0 to City – but they weren't done yet. Momentum can be a huge factor in the outcome of a football match, and City were determined to keep it up.

Despite a Birmingham substitution – Lucy Quinn coming on for Gemma Lawley in defence – City soon doubled their lead.

Chloe broke at pace down the right wing, receiving the ball from midfield, before dancing past the newly introduced Quinn, who wasn't yet up to speed.

Chloe whipped a delightful cross into the box, which was met by Lauren Hemp – who rifled it into the net.

Now City had two. In the space of just 15 minutes, Chloe had helped swing the game firmly in City's favour.

Now Birmingham's resolve was broken. They knew they had no response to the City play, and could only hope it wouldn't get worse.

Just three minutes later, a scramble in the box left Georgia with an open net. She didn't need asking twice and tapped it home.

City had scored three goals in six minutes.

With the game well and truly finished as a contest, and with just 20 minutes remaining, City made four substitutions. There were other important games coming up, and Gareth Taylor wanted to rest players to be fit for them.

But there was only one thing on Chloe's mind. Sarina Wiegman would be watching this game, with a view to selecting England players – so Chloe needed to impress. She needed to make this a memorable performance.

Moments after the City substitutions, the ball broke to Chloe on the edge of the penalty area, following a City corner. She whipped in a dangerous cross, which fell at the back post to Alanna Kennedy – who couldn't miss with her header.

Now City had four – and Chloe had two assists. All she needed now was a goal to cap off an incredible second-half display.

With less than ten minutes remaining, she finally got the goal she deserved. Lauren Hemp played a pinpoint through-ball, splitting the Birmingham defence, before Chloe strode onto it and smashed it into the roof of the net.

In that moment, Chloe was able – finally – to let go of the last remnants of doubt surrounding her injury.

She'd shown that she was strong, fresh, and better than ever. Her injuries were in the past.

Now she had plenty to look forward to – the FA Cup final, and the promise of being in the England squad for the Euros.

Birmingham conceded a sixth goal in the dying embers of the game, rounding off an incredible second-half display from City.

Chloe had come into the game at 0-0 and, in 45 minutes, had played a pivotal role in completely dismantling Birmingham.

It was plain for everyone to see – Chloe was getting back to her best, and Chloe at her best was unstoppable.

She could only hope that Sarina Wiegman had been paying close attention.

18
LIONESS

February 2023, Ashton Gate, Bristol, England
Arnold Clark Cup, England v Belgium

"So how does it feel to be England royalty?" Alessia Russo asked Chloe excitedly.

"It still hasn't quite sunk in yet," Chloe laughed.

"Well, we're going to need some more of your magic today," Alessia smiled.

It was the evening of England's final game in the Arnold Clark Cup, against Belgium, and the Lionesses were in good spirits. They knew that avoiding defeat tonight would win them the trophy – retaining the title from the first year of the tournament, in 2022.

It would also take them to a 29-game unbeaten run.

It had been an incredible past year for England – and for Chloe in particular.

Following her recovery from injury, her sparkling form for Man City had been enough to convince Sarina Wiegman that Chloe deserved a place in her Euro 2022 squad.

Chloe had more than paid back the trust from her manager. That image of Chloe, wheeling away in celebration, shirt aloft, being mobbed by her team-mates, after scoring the Euro-winning goal against Germany, late in extra time …

That image had gone viral. Chloe had become an icon.

It was all so surreal. On the treatment table, at the lowest point of her ACL recovery, Chloe would never have believed that all this would be possible. But she'd come back stronger than ever, writing herself into football's history books.

Today, Chloe had the chance to continue England's winning streak, as well as to retain the Arnold Clark Cup. This was an invitational tournament, nowhere near as important as the Euros – but, to Chloe, it was still significant.

Most of her England team-mates had been in the Arnold Clark Cup-winning squad of 2022, but Chloe had missed out, owing to her injury. So she wanted to win the cup this year.

England's opponents were Belgium. They were the lowest of the four teams in the FIFA rankings, but so far had dispatched both Italy and South Korea with ease – just as England had done.

This meant that both England and Belgium were tied on six points – with this, the deciding match, being a winner-takes-all affair.

Chloe had played many games against weaker teams, and she knew never to underestimate an opponent just because, on paper, they appeared weaker. Football is not played on paper, and she knew that anything can happen in the 90 minutes on the pitch.

Chloe was starting the match – her Euros heroics had

made sure of that – and, as she stood in the tunnel, she could hear the excited buzz of the Ashton Gate crowd.

The Lionesses had brought women's football to the attention of a much wider audience in England. Now everyone knew their names and were eager to support the team. Chloe wanted to go out and put on a show for them.

Sarina gave some words of encouragement to the players as they assembled in the tunnel, but her main message to them was just to go out and enjoy themselves.

With the World Cup in Australia and New Zealand due to start in July, this match was England's chance to show the world that they were still at the top of their game.

England's reputation had preceded them and, as the match kicked off, Chloe could see that Belgium were nervous. They were hesitant, and struggled early on to deal with the skill of the England forwards.

Chloe would pick the ball up in midfield and surge toward the Belgium backline, who were obviously afraid to tackle her, knowing that Chloe could jink one way or the other at any time, forcing them to commit a foul.

Only 12 minutes in, Belgium's caution came back to bite them. Lauren James went on a mazy run into the box and, sensing the danger before any of the Belgium defenders, Chloe dropped to the back post.

Lauren played a perfect cross, which the defenders fumbled in an attempted clearance, before Chloe pounced on their indecision and put England into the lead.

England dominated the rest of the first half, and five minutes before the half-time whistle, they managed to grab a second goal.

Lucy Bronze whipped in a perfect cross and Leah Williamson rose highest to nod home.

England had played the perfect half in front of the near sell-out Ashton Gate crowd. Belgium simply couldn't match the level of England's play and hadn't managed to get a single shot on target.

Five minutes into the second half, the Belgium keeper, Nicky Evrard, palmed an England shot straight into the danger zone – where Chloe was lurking.

Chloe made no mistake and put England into a 3-0 lead.

"You know you're in the lead for the Golden Boot now, right?" Alessia said, hugging Chloe amidst the goal celebrations.

"I've already got a space for it in the trophy cabinet," Chloe laughed.

Chloe had scored a goal in the opening match against South Korea and, with the two against Belgium, she now stood at the top of the scoring table.

The rest of the match followed in the same way. Belgium were simply outclassed by England and, at the final whistle, England ran out 6-1 winners.

Not only had they trounced the competition – they'd put on a spectacular show for the England fans.

Now nobody could have any doubt that England would be one of the favourites going into the 2023 World Cup. They'd retained the Arnold Clark Cup with three wins out of three matches, improving on 2022's performance of one win and two draws.

The Lionesses had conquered European football – now it was the world stage that awaited them.

And Chloe had proved beyond any doubt that she was one of the best players in the world. Yet she was still only 25 years old. The peak of her career was still some way away.

Despite having achieved so much already, Chloe was still determined to prove herself to the world.

She was going to make sure that, at the World Cup in July, the whole world would know her name.

Chloe Kelly.

And she would not let them forget it.

HOW MANY HAVE YOU READ?

- MESSI — Harry Coninx
- KELLY — Robin Adams
- HAALAND — Harry Coninx
- RONALDO (New Updated Edition) — Harry Coninx
- SALAH — Harry Coninx
- PULISIC — Harry Coninx
- KANE — Harry Coninx
- NEYMAR — Matt Carver
- MBAPPÉ — Harry Coninx
- SON — Harry Coninx
- SAKA — Harry Coninx
- LEWANDOWSKI (New Updated Edition) — Harry Coninx
- FÉLIX — Harry Coninx
- GNABRY — Harry Coninx
- STERLING — Harry Coninx
- RASHFORD (New Updated Edition) — Harry Coninx
- KANTÉ — Harry Coninx
- SILVA — Harry Coninx
- VAN DIJK — Harry Coninx
- MAHREZ — Harry Coninx
- SANCHO — Harry Coninx
- KLOPP — Harry Coninx
- SOUTHGATE — Harry Coninx
- GUARDIOLA — Harry Coninx